AF254677

Long Hair, Do Care

The Black Girl's Ultimate Cheat Sheet
for **Growing Long Healthy Hair**

YVETTE BRASWELL

Published by Yvette Braswell and YBM Productions;
ISBN- 978-1-64007-461-3
Cover Art: Sherrill Defoe

Acknowledgements

First To God for blessing me beyond belief and making me a part of the ALL

To my ancestors- May the circle be unbroken

To My Parents, Dorothy and John Braswell- A million thanks could never be too much. Love you both to the moon and back. RIP Daddy

To TJ (My Woo) for making me better

To My Family and Friends- Because you always support my movements

To My Clients for confirming that my gift wasn't an illusion

To The Hair Game- Because it's always been good to me

To Dennis Ross (Editor)- Thanks for being patient with me.

To Sherrill Defoe (Cover Artist)- Thank you for your brilliant artistry on the cover.

To everyone holding this book, I pray in the spirit of thanks, that you and your passion for hair (whether for private or professional reasons) never stops growing, both literally and figuratively.

Contents

Long Hair, Do Care

The Black Girl's Ultimate Cheat Sheet
for **Growing Long Healthy Hair**

Introduction

Long Hair, Do Care- *A Black Girl's Ultimate Cheat Sheet for Growing Long Healthy Hair* is a very short book that will get you to the bottom line- Mo' HAIR. I call it a cheat sheet, because in the spirit of Cliff Notes and answer keys, it cuts out all of the fluff and gets right to the point. This book was written to walk you through growing your hair *the easy way*. There are times when I will get a little technical, but don't worry. It's only for you to have a better understanding of what you're working with. I want you to read this Long Hair, Do Care from beginning to end, to get the full benefit of what's in store for you. However, there are no rules to this reading thing. So, feel free to skip around, read through, or focus on very specific information. Either way you slice it, you're going to grow your hair.

Although I believe a true hairstylist should do ALL hair types (regardless of texture, and no matter the race of the person), in Long Hair, Do Care, *A Black Girl's Ultimate Cheat Sheet for Long, Healthy Hair,* I'm choosing to focus on Black women. For years, I have seen how intense and deep-seated the desire is for us to have long hair. I've seen the 'real Black girls' with long hair being questioned as to how they got their weave to look so natural (as if long hair is not even a possibility for us). I've witnessed how, when a Black woman wants long hair, she's accused of wanting to be 'White'- like Black women can't maintain their 'Blackness' and have long straight hair that swings well beyond her bra straps… Like we don't have a right to choose what texture we want to rock without our 'Black Card' possibly being questioned, if not pulled. Whether natural or processed, it's time to change the narrative in regards to Black women and long hair. I mean, do your thing however you need to. Wear a weave or a relaxer, if you want. Wear natural hair if you choose. But, don't let people put you into a 'bag' about how to express yourself and your culture. <u>Do YOU</u>. This long hair is for 'us' too. It's more important to be Black on the inside than on the outside.

How did this book come about???
My dear friend (and one of my most reliable confidents), Meredith Harper-Houston, is constantly encouraging me to push to my limits. If I come to her with an idea, she will have a million suggestions on how to make it as awesome as humanly possible. She's a big part of the reason this book has come to be. We met, maybe 15 years or so ago, and since then, she has been telling me that there is a book somewhere in my story. "Hmmm… that does sound like a good idea. But, 'about what?' is the question," was always my response. Neither of us really had an idea of what the book should be about, but we both felt like there were definitely some stories to be told. The one thing I knew for sure was that I wanted to write about something I knew inside out. I would have to be myself while telling the story. Now, one million years later, I have finally come up with my first work. Of course, it turned out to be about hair! At first, I was going to call this book 'Yvette B's travels in Hairy Tale Land,' because I thought it was cute. But, it didn't really speak to what I wanted you to know, I just thought it was 'cute.' Then, I really thought about, polled about, and researched about the information Black women wanted to know most, in regards to their hair. All roads kept leading to 'We want *long* and *healthy*!' Therefore, I had to make like the O'Jays, and give the people what they want. I also needed to keep all of the information very short, sweet, and to the point, as

to not be a total snooze-fest. Maybe calling it a cheat sheet would be a nice twist, because the readers would be able to skip straight to the answers and get A+ results (How cool is that???). Thus, the title- Long Hair, Do Care- The Black Girl's Ultimate Cheat Sheet for Long Healthy Hair was born.

I want to give a shout out to all the civilians who are reading this book purely for vanity's sake. *Whoo! whooo!!* You're cooking with gas now! I won't go too hard on you for your prior hair crimes and misdemeanors; because you all were doing what you thought was right. Bless your hearts. No more winging it loves! Let *Long Hair, Do Care* be *your* personal road map to lengths never before reached. Tools like this book, YouTube, and Google are wonderful references, guides, and resources that go hand in hand with professional salon visits. I often use these tools myself, when I'm stuck on how to get a style done. But, my belief in the power of seeing a real deal hair artist is serious. It's a super important element of maintaining long, healthy hair. The stylist who really floats your boat may not be easy to find. But she/he will be worth the effort. Listen, I know the plight of the girl out there reading the books, articles, and websites, trying to get to the power hair. Even with all of your research, you sometimes still end up with questions, AND hair that falls short of your goals. *Long Hair, Do Care* will help you to know what to do, and to recognize what to look for in a stylist. I tried to put everything I thought you might need in here. If I've missed anything you feel I should have covered, feel free to shoot me an email, or come to a book reading, and let's talk it out. Oh! And, send me pictures of your progress. I'd love to see the results of you following the steps in this book! Now, I'm not promising the information here will turn you into an overnight cosmetologist or Rapunzel, but it *will* make whatever you and your stylist come up with during your regular visits more effective. The foundation of your stylist's work will be SO much sturdier when you follow a hair ritual and do your part at home. (Not doing *too* much, though... *just* doing your part). Your hairstyles will last longer, look better, you'll cut out the hours lost to guess work and research, and you'll eventually have long, healthy, hair.

So, on to our Long Hair, Do Care Hairy Tale Land adventure! Let me forewarn you: I really like to let my hair down (no pun intended) and be myself- Especially when I'm talking about something I love. Think of me as your good-good girlfriend who's spilling all of the hair tea. I want you to feel both comfortable and well informed. I have a great feeling about our new relationship. I'm all giddy and stuff! Long, healthy, hair will be the trophy of your commitment to following the guidelines in this book. I'm going to share the secrets I've learned in my 25+ years as a student, an expert, a salon owner, and an entertainment industry hair professional with you. My years of pocket curls, pin ups, and hair extensions, have taught me that, as a hair care professional, you are only as good as the mistakes you can correct (trust me, I learned this truth the hard way!). I want the best for you. Anyone can *do hair-* But not everyone can grow it. Guess who's about to be a hair-growing machine? YOU!

Mo' Hair!

For Panesha and I, hair created an unbreakable bond. One far beyond the beauty of a great "do." In many ways, hair saved our lives. You see, the client-stylist relationship is an interesting one. What can start out as professional relationship can quickly turn into a therapeutic connection; a relationship where you establish the trust to discuss everything, and I do mean everything. You can start out doing hair, and end up doing life together. We had so much in common. For example, Panesha shares the same birthday as my mother. I can't count how many times I would start a sentence about a date, and she would finish it having had a similar experience. Collectively, we had probably kissed enough frogs to fill a zoo! We had run the full gamut of the good and the bad. Plus, we both knew the pain of losing our fathers.

The second she walked in the door of the salon, I could tell what kind of week it had been. Her days were spent looking after her ill father, while working, and taking care of her special-needs daughter. For a normal person, this would have taken its toll, but it all seemed to roll off her back. Somehow, some way, "Nesh," as I affectionately call her, kept the most positive outlook during the most difficult of times. So on that special day, I couldn't have been happier to be a part of making her look as beautiful on the outside as she is on the inside. We were in New Orleans, and she was about to get married to the man of her dreams. Standing there beside her, I couldn't help but remember all we'd been through together. This moment was huge! What she didn't know was she was not only giving me hope, but the two of us there together was confirmation that faith moves mountains. I had no idea when she walked into the salon for her first appointment that a simple shampoo and style would lead to her being one of my truest friends. The bond between client and stylist is truly a unique one.

Hair is more than beauty. Hair is healing. Hair is hope. As stylists, we go through the good, the bad and the ugly with our clients. Those few hours we spend give us both the chance to let go and bounce feelings, ideas, and dreams off of one another.

For all the vanity and misplaced importance around having beautiful hair (natural or weave), one thing is often overlooked. Hair changes lives. There's nothing more fulfilling than working with a client to unlock the door to grow her hair into a healthy mane. I've had the privilege to do this many times, with many other clients. When I help a woman reach her 'hair goals,' the reward is far more than business; it's purpose. When we look good, we feel better. And when we feel better, in a small way, we make the world a better place. For right or wrong, a woman's confidence is rooted in her hair. Hair matters.

Being a hairstylist has been my expression, my provider, my outlet, and my rock. At times in my life when I didn't know what to do or where to turn, my work was always there. My "Hairy Tale" journey, as I like to call it, has opened doors I never even imagined. Hair has allowed me everything from meeting my idol, Muhammad Ali, to being hired to work on a project for Presidential Candidate Hillary Clinton. When I was just a little girl running around my daddy's hair salon and doing cartwheels, I never imagined all of the things my trade would help me achieve. Hair styling has enhanced my world immensely. It has given me the confidence to know that anything I want to do is possible. It will always be a part of who I am, no matter what else I do.

~~~
~~~

This book is not only an ode to the love I have always had for hair, but it is also my contribution to the standard of excellence for which we hair care professionals and fans of awesome hair should be striving. Anyone who knows me well knows that I have lived and breathed the beauty industry my entire life. My love affair with all things hair and beauty is something that has never let me down. My Dad, lovingly known by most as 'Mr. John,' owned a salon before I was born, and I literally started working in it by the age of 8. It was then I discovered that hair and I were automatic. Eventually, I moved all the way through the salon ranks- from garbage girl, to assistant, eventually to owner, and every role in between (please don't be afraid to start at the bottom, love bunnies!). Learning as much as I could about hair and how to make it grow out as shiny and beautifully as possible, has always been my passion. As I matured as a stylist and continued to learn, I developed a thing that some people call 'growing hands' (the ability to make *anyone's* hair grow). Being rather naïve, I assumed all hairdressers had both the ability and burning curiosity about the craft. As time went on, I'll admit that I became disenchanted with the discovery that this was not the case. Not every stylist loves this work with her/his heart and soul, or takes the time to learn how to become her/his best self. There are levels to the hair game, and to some, the business of hair is just that - **business**. I've seen a-many-a- snatched out edges, breakage, and bald spots from the relentless pursuit of hang time. And I'm not talking about civilians or do it yourself-ers wandering through the beauty supplies. We're talking about 'PROFESSIONALS'! **BEWARE love bunnies**!!!

Some folks are in it for the bread and not the head (I just made that up! LOL!). Let me say that again, some folks are in it for the bread and not the head! Meaning, they don't care about ethics or the well-being of your hair. They care exclusively about swiping your card or counting your cash. I know I'm not alone when I say I can't even count the times I have had to come behind a person who refused to admit she/he didn't have the education to healthily get to the client to the desired style. Some stylists (not you, of course) just don't have the patience or proper training to explain to a client WHY for what she wants is not what was best for her. Maybe it is the fear of upsetting the client, or losing the money. Either way, it's time to bring all of that to a close. Honesty is the best policy. I've yet to lose a client from telling the truth about the consequences of doing something unhealthy or unsafe to her hair. Even if the client goes to someone else to get a 'yes' 9 times out of 10 they come back after the damage has been done. Don't get me wrong though- as stylists, when we can't give the client what she thinks she wants, it's our responsibility to have a fresh alternative to the request. This means (stylists) get your weight up.

Don't be a one trick hair pony, who can only do color *OR* hair extensions...or whatever. You don't have to be an expert in all things hair. However, taking continuing education can make you very fluid behind the chair. It will save your clients both hair and time, and it will add substantially to your income (*cha-ching!*). #NO LIMITS. I'm sure there will be plenty of days when even the best stylist won't feel like being everything to everybody. You may not even feel like getting up to go to work. You might be looking forward to the last head of the day (with achy feet). But, when you love the art and want what's best for the client, you get the knowledge and give your best (*much love to you all!*). To the clients who are reading- that's the stylist you want to pick. Choose the one you can really feel how much she/he cares about you, and your hair. If you're a stylist, you're blessed to support yourself while doing what you love! This comes with a big responsibility. *Stay Hungry.*

For the record, I will not be discussing product brands, or suggesting, or instructing, on how to achieve different hairstyles…That might be on the next go round. What I will reveal, are the tried and true methods that will get you to achieve your long hair goals. We're going from the bottom to the top with all of the essentials you need, from supplies, to-do lists, how to care for your children's hair, and even a 12 week 'cheat sheet'/schedule of *when* you should be doing *what* to your hair. I've even managed to get a few of my really busy Celebrity Hairstylist friends to chime in with some of their secrets for growing long, healthy, hair. Get ready for the full shebang-bang!

I'm known, affectionately, to most of my clients as "Yvette B Hair GURU" and I humbly accept and appreciate the title (even though I put my government name on the cover). I read somewhere that in Hindu Sanskrit 'guru' means 'the remover of darkness.' I can roll with that, because I've always been passionate about hair, and I enjoy shedding light on all things having to do with it. My goal is for *Long Hair, Do Care* to start a HAIRVOLUTION, and become the go-to guide for Black women and girls all around the world. A guide for all those who wish for their hair to reach amazing lengths. I'm *super* grateful my clients and colleagues have stamped me with their seal of approval, and I'm doing my best to live up to the title. More than anything, I'm glad to have the opportunity to share what I know about hair with you. So, strap up and let's take a quick journey through 'Hairy Tale Land'.

Disclaimer

THIS BOOK IS NOT DESIGNED TO, AND DOES NOT, PROVIDE MEDICAL ADVICE. ALL CONTENT ("CONTENT"), INCLUDING TEXT, GRAPHICS, IMAGES AND INFORMATION AVAILABLE IN THIS BOOK ARE FOR GENERAL INFORMATIONAL PURPOSES ONLY.
THE CONTENT IS NOT INTENDED TO BE A SUBSTITUTE FOR PROFESSIONAL MEDICAL ADVICE, DIAGNOSIS OR TREATMENT. NEVER DISREGARD PROFESSIONAL MEDICAL ADVICE, OR DELAY SEEKING IT, BECAUSE OF SOMETHING YOU HAVE READ IN THIS BOOK. NEVER RELY ON INFORMATION IN THIS BOOK IN PLACE OF SEEKING PROFESSIONAL MEDICAL ADVICE. LONG HAIR, DO CARE (A BLACK WOMAN'S ULTIMATE CHEAT SHEET FOR GROWING LONG HEALTHY HAIR) IS NOT RESPONSIBLE OR LIABLE FOR ANY ADVICE, COURSE OF TREATMENT, DIAGNOSIS OR ANY OTHER INFORMATION, SERVICES OR PRODUCTS THAT YOU OBTAIN THROUGH THIS BOOK. YOU ARE ENCOURAGED TO CONFER WITH YOUR DOCTOR WITH REGARD TO INFORMATION CONTAINED IN OR THROUGH THIS BOOK. AFTER READING THIS BOOK AND CONTENT THEREOF, YOU ARE ENCOURAGED TO REVIEW THE INFORMATION CAREFULLY WITH YOUR PROFESSIONAL HEALTHCARE PROVIDER.

IMPORTANT MESSAGE: **This book is not a license or an instruction manual to STOP seeing a professional hairstylist**.

Let's Get It Started!

MC Hammer was definitely on to something when he made that statement! So, you want to grow long healthy hair? Maybe you already have long hair, but you feel you've hit a brick wall in your growth. Or, maybe you're a hair artist who wants to grow in your craft. You may even be a curious hairstylist who wants to see if I know what the hell I'm talking about… You know- see if there is any useful information in this here Long Hair, Do Care business. Whoever you may be, I welcome you. I came here to show and prove. YOU WILL GROW THIS HAIR. I have been both blessed and lucky to be able to have amazing hair mentors, artists, and co-workers throughout my career. Without having been taught so much by so many, I would never have become who I am now. I realize a lot of my education came from both being under the right teachers, stationed next to the right stylists, and in the right salon at the right time. I've been fortunate enough to get a million dollar education for pennies on the dollar. I want to give you this information as freely as it was given to me.

Whether your hair is chemically processed or natural, I can guarantee that if you work the plan and follow the blueprint in these pages, it will take a little time, but the results will show. Just be patient and stick with it. I have high hopes for you, dear reader. I said before I want this book to be your "hands on" reference material for all things *LONG, HEALTHY* hair, and doggone it- I mean it! Keep Long Hair, Do Care right by your side in your Kindle, notebook, or your cell phone, to guide you through the mazes of Hairy Tale Land. My goal is to eliminate having to do a google search to know simple facts about your hair like: How often you need a trim, or which types of conditioners you need for your hair, or any combination of other long hair questions you may have. Away with all of the confusion! We're doing a simple regimen. I'll let you in on a little secret, too- *Even if you really want short hair, all of this information still works. You'll just get to be walking around with amazingly healthy and beautiful hair that you choose to cut!*

To the Clients/Civilians-
Even without having met you, I'm willing to bet there have been many times you've found yourself leaving the salon with no real instructions to follow when you get home. Stuck all up in Hairy Tale Land without the Rapunzel recipe! Be honest with me... Have you ever been at the salon and had the feeling you were being shuffled? You know that thing your stylist sometimes does when she/he condemns you to the dryer, so she/he can hurry up and get on the phone or IPad? In all honesty, sometimes we need to sit you down somewhere so we can attack those hot wings that have been sitting on the station getting cold, for the last hour. To that I say, NEVER AGAIN! Oh yes, you may be on your way to the dryer, but both YOU and the stylist will have the understanding as to why. You're about to get real fancy, Boo. You will no longer just be getting styled and sent on- all in the dark... without having been advised of, or not *really* understanding your hair homework. You may even come out of your face with some questions about what's going on- 'Is this week that I'm supposed to get a masque or the deep conditioner?' Or, 'What about a trim this week?' You may even hit her/him with the, 'What products do YOU recommend for me to handle A,B, & C problem?,' and 'What do you recommend I do at home to maintain my hair?' If your stylist even flinches on any of these questions, you have

some quick decisions to make. Read below and pick what is the right answer.

1.   Find a cute way to give your stylist this book and tell her/him to get to studying?
2.   Fire your stylist and get someone who REALLY knows their stuff?
3.   Take matters into your own hands and be a do-it-yourselfer until you can get to safety?
4.   All of the above

Oh yes, we're about to shake some stuff up with this book, honey! Please know this; by no means am I telling you to be shady to your stylist. Please be kind and loving with your new information. Don't go trying to call your stylist out about every little thing (I know how you all can be with new-found information sometimes!). If you see her/him slipping, please be kind with your suggestions. Let's spread good vibes everywhere we go with this healthy hair thing.

To the Professional Stylists-
I truly appreciate you supporting me and buying my book. Hopefully, we're kindred spirits, in as much as you love life in Hairy Tale Land as much as me. I visualize you out there on the front lines working to give people those wonderful styles they desire. Welcome teammate! I'm glad you have trusted me enough to give Long Hair, Do Care a whirl. Let's have a circle of trust moment- do you feel like there's more do know? Have you been investing in your continuing education? Could you stand to stretch yourself to make more money? If the answer is yes, I'm glad this book can be a piece to your puzzle. As stylists, sometimes we can become very comfortable with getting by with doing

the same things over and over, and not really paying attention to what our clients need. You know- doing just enough to 'get by' and pay the bills, but not enough to boldly step into new, fresh territory. How many times have you stood shoulder-to-shoulder with your beauty school classmates or your co-workers who can barely get through the chemistry section of that cosmetology book, or don't know jack about *any* type of complex chemical processes? You know the ones who only know enough to get through State Board and into the salon, but when it comes down to doing anything past making the clients 'cute' they're at a loss. Isn't it sad? You don't have to call the person out, just do a little mental picture with a check mark by it. The time has come to stop faking it, for both the clients and our own sakes. *Can we put them on the 'gift' list, and un-shadily shoot them a copy of Long Hair, Do Care?* I'm just saying… Life can hold beautiful surprises, when we step outside of our comfort zones.

My hope is that Long Hair, Do Care is one of the tools that ignites the flame to usher you into your zone of genius, where your work is pleasure and knowledge is power. Kudos for watering your seeds, big ups for walking the talk, and being serious about your business. We're at the crossroads separating talent and competence, from developing your skill set and leveling up from passion to expertise.

As an exceptional stylist you:
1. Are up on what's current and cutting edge.
2. Know how to keep your clients hair growing.
3. Have clients with amazing, healthy hair that attracts you even <u>more</u> clientele.

4.   Don't have to spend up appointment time being constantly directed on what needs to be done by the person in the chair.
5.   Discover and prescribe (Hello, hair doctor!).
6.   Understand why quality products are essential to long, healthy hair.
7.   Have clients that wear extension because they want to, not because they have to.
8.   Know the Betty Ferguson rule- "The magic happens at the shampoo bowl."

I, by no means, want to discount a bomb hairstylist. We know the finished product is what we *live* for. But, when we neglect treatment services, we are doing our clients, our reputations as stylists, and our pockets a disservice. I am enthused about the possibilities for your career. Integrating a client maintenance regimen into your service creates opportunity for not only stepping up your finished product and keeping your clients coming back, but also for up-selling and securing your future. By default, your product knowledge increases (because you'll switch up products every so often, remembering that even the best stuff becomes ineffective after so much use. ***When the bottle runs dry, find a new supply!). As a a great stylist, I know that's what you're about. You will always be in discovery mode, in regards to your hair potions and creative abilities. You'll either find some quality products that speak to your methods of styling, or you'll create them. All the while your client list will be growing. So will their hair.

3 Simple Rules for Having Long Healthy Hair

There are actually two, #1 rules of having long healthy hair. We'll call them rules #1a and #1b. Rule #1a is to give your hair moisture, Moisture, and **MOISTURE!** It is essential to the survival of a Black woman's hair. Even though our hair is typically made up of 6% moisture already, the daily wear and tear we give it means we must always be working towards maintaining what's there. Your silk scarf is an essential tool for keeping your hair together. While you sleep or hang out around the house, it performs a mini hot oil treatment. Mind you, it must be 100% silk, because any other fabric will only draw moisture <u>out</u>. Nope... a satin pillowcase WILL NOT DO. You'll notice after you've slept on one, that the oil from your hair and skin are all over it. It's completely opposite from how your 100% silk scarf looks when you take it off and start your day. Remember, there are absolutely no substitutes for 100% silk.

For many Black girls, there are definite misconceptions as to what a moisturized head actually means. Sebum (your hair's natural oil) serves as a protective substance that prevents the hair from drying out or absorbing excessive amounts of external substances. It can be distributed down the hair shaft "mechanically" by brushing and combing. But, sometimes our hair doesn't produce as much sebum necessary by itself, and we have to help the hair out with our products. That is where your oils and conditioners come in. We have to apply these products externally to make up for what is missing naturally and replace the sebum you would otherwise be producing.

There's also this thing called porosity we have to deal with. When the hair becomes super dry, it typically means it's highly porous. Porous hair has raised cuticles that will not hold moisture within its internal layer, known as the cortex. Dryness simply means the moisture in the cortex has dissolved. Where the problem lies is that the natural bond of the hair (on the outside) has been broken down, leaving the inside parts vulnerable. Any damage or changes made to the visible hair shaft cannot be repaired naturally, but the cuticle can definitely be managed. Imagine your hair shaft has a million little half opened umbrellas lined up, one over the next, all the way down its length. In order to protect what's under the umbrella, you would have to rebuild the protein bonds by applying a protein reconstructive conditioner. This would serve as the equivalent of closing the umbrellas completely to protect the inner layers. Now here's the rub... Protein (reconstructive conditioner) dries the hair out. So, it must be immediately followed by an extremely moisturizing conditioner and a leave-in. Those two products work as softening agents that come through after the protein has done the hard work. **NEVER USE A PROTEIN CONDITIONER BY ITSELF.** ALWAYS, ALWAYS, ALWAYS follow up with a moisturizing deep conditioning treatment. Or, you WILL be looking like Cap'n Crunch by the head! Many women believe the misconception that grease, oil sheen, and silicone shine products equal moisture. No ma'am! These are styling products. They do nothing for the actual structure of the hair shaft, where the real healing takes place. I won't get into all of the technicalities and science of how hair works, right now, but I will say this. We don't want to be faking our hair out with products that coat our hair with a temporary layer of shine.

Healthy hair will shine even before you add styling products. Healthy hair = Long hair.

***Note to the ladies who work out:

> *I know your hair feels icky when you work out and sweat in your head. It makes you want to shampoo your hair every day. Please resist! When you shampoo your hair, you remove precious sebum your body has created for it, which helps to keep it from breaking. I know it's hard. But I'm going to have to say- Shampoo once a week.*

This may be to your surprise, but rule #1b is actually the easiest instruction, but the hardest one for people to follow. It is this: **LEAVE YOUR HAIR ALONE**. Let this statement settle in for a bit. Everything about your hair wants to grow, naturally. As long as your hair follicles and bulbs are not damaged, your hair is *going* to grow. The key to getting long hair is keeping what has grown from your scalp on your head, for the duration of its life cycle. When unbothered, hair can reach amazing lengths! Alright… alright- Of course, you have to do *something* to your hair to maintain it, but, not an overabundance of things. The goal is to keep your routine as simple as you can, while maintaining your polished look. Realistically, you can't leave your hair *completely* alone. Please don't! Lord knows, there is nothing I loathe more than a girl with a raggedy head! I love you all and everything… but if I see another Naturalista who thinks natural means 'no maintenance, somebody may have to call the authorities on me. I'll be somewhere yelling:

> *"Girl, don't be giving the 'fro a bad name!... If you don't prep your hair at night…! OMG!…This is visual homicide!...*

Your WHOLE head is not supposed to look like the root, though."

My bad- I got carried away (no shade to the fly natural girls, PURE shade to the aforementioned). What I'm trying to say is, there is no such thing as zero maintenance. Being lazy about your look is *'no Bueno.'* We all know that if your hair (and shoes) looks bad, it doesn't matter how cute all of the rest of your ensemble is, you're *DONE.* At any rate, get a good trim and shape to your hair, keep your hair moist, follow your regimen (using great products), tie your hair up at night, and see your stylist. That's how simple you want to keep your hair life.

Rule #3 (short and sweet) is to *follow a hair treatment routine* you don't have to even think about. In this routine, you commit to following it, while purposely doing as little as possible to your hair. Why? Because, the less you do to your hair, the more your hair will do for you.

I want to be very clear in stating this book is not made to eliminate the need to go see your professional hairstylist. Ain't nothing like having a real artist do what they do. Long Hair, Do Care was made to go hand in hand with the investment you have made in the overall health of your hair. I recommend seeing your stylist at least once a month, but, if you go once a week or every two weeks that's fine. All of this information still applies. When we get in the habit of fiddling with our hair on a regular basis, we are normally doing more harm than good. Styling products can become an obstacle course of what to use, and when. Many of them contain ingredients that are more complex than we expect, and experimenting with them can lead to fallout (both major and minor). Consulting with your stylist about products and styles is never a bad idea. The 'Cheat

Sheet' at the end of this book, which is to be used along with your silk scarf and the instructions your stylist gives you, removes the need to do a bunch of guesswork with the precious hair you are growing. In a nutshell, your job at home will be maintaining whatever your hairstylist has done for you until the next time you see her/him.

The Facts of Hair

I'm sure we've all heard the hair cons before. You know, the magic potion or tool able to grow your hair two inches in an hour… or a week… or a month. Just like the magic drink that melts 15 pounds off your body while you sleep within three days, without exercise, and without giving up the midnight blueberry cheesecake. LIES! LIES! I say!!! No matter what the 'experts' promise, hair is only going to naturally grow about ¼ of an inch per month. You might get ½ of an inch if you're lucky. The reality is, there are no quick fixes to genetics. The good news is this, if you can keep from seriously damaging your follicles, the possibility for long hair is always there. That being said, there are two important things you need to know to achieve maximum length:

1) What your hair is made of, and 2) The growth cycle of each strand. Knowing the facts of hair makes it not so scary when you see a few strands on the floor. Knowledge is POWER ladies!

WARNING: Hold on to your seat! We're about to get a little scientific.

Let's do a breakdown of each part of the strand, because it's important you understand *what* you're actually preserving with all of the information you're getting from Long Hair, Do Care. We don't want all of these products and treatments you invest to be in vain! We need all roads lead to your hair bangin' and slangin'.

So, let's begin-

The hair structure is made up of three parts:
- *Cuticle (outer layer)*
- *Cortex (middle layer)*

- *Medulla (the core center layer)*

The cuticle is a very critical layer of your hair. Its purpose is to protect the cortex and medulla. It has a stacked scaly appearance and acts in an umbrella-like function over the layers that it protects. Like an umbrella, the scales point towards the ends of the hair and are opened to different degrees up and down the hair shaft. The cuticle controls the water content of the hair's inner structure, and is affected by every product you put on your hair. When chemicals and products are strong enough, they can either lift the cuticle and get under it, causing changes to the structure of the hair, or close it down causing the hair to have a smoothed out, shiny finish. Because textured hair has naturally raised cuticles, particular care has to be taken with it to maintain moisture.

The cortex layer of the hair shaft is where the color of your hair (melanin) lives. It is directly affected by hair color, shampoos, and conditioners. The cuticle lies directly over the cortex as a shield. Gray hair also has a cortex, but it's missing melanin. This precious layer is responsible for the texture and muscle in your hair. A very important responsibility of the cortex is to surround and protect the medulla. When damage or changes are made to the cortex they can't be undone, which is why it's so important to treat your hair tenderly. However, if you slip and beat your hair up a little, all is not lost. The good news is that the cuticle can be maneuvered in a way to protect the damaged interior of the strand, allowing it to live it's full life span with a healthy appearance.

Last but not least, is the medulla (the inner most layer of the hair strand). It is usually only present in thick hair. The medulla can be likened to marrow in the bones (giving vitality and strength). Blondes don't have this layer as part of their hair shaft. It is not a necessary layer for the hair to be considered healthy, but it does add to its body.

Whew! That was an eye full, now wasn't it ladies??? Well, we're not quite done with science class just yet. Now, we have to get to the 'how long your hair actually *stays* on your head' part. I'm so glad that when I told my good, good, girlfriend (former salon owner/stylist Myla Beal), that I was writing a book on long hair, she reminded me of just how important it was for the readers to know about **SHEDDING,** and where it fits into the growth cycle. Many women panic when they see <u>any</u> of their hair on the floor. But, losing a few strands here and there is not always a bad thing. Now don't get me wrong, if you can't see your bathroom floor for the hair not he ground, then we have a problem! Understanding how much hair is actually healthy to lose, can ease your mind and help you along in your journey of growth.

There are three phases in the growth cycle of a strand of hair: *ANAGEN, CATAGEN, and TELOGEN.* Let's talk about it.

In the ANAGEN PHASE, your hair grows about a ½ an inch per month. It remains on your head anywhere from of 3-7 years, giving the strand the potential to grow up to 18-30 inches (Ladies, imagine keeping all of that lovely length!).

The CATAGEN PHASE is the short transitional period of about 10 days, where God's magic is happening, that takes the hair into its' final telogen state.

Finally, when the hair reaches its' TELOGEN PHASE, it is at a place of rest, just on the verge of shedding from the follicle. Once the fall out has happened, the follicle stays inactive for 90 days, and the process starts all over again.

So, the goal is to get to the 18-30 inches as gorgeously as humanly possible! Again, this is why the cheat sheet is essential. The beauty I've found in the three cycles is that each follicle individually goes through its metamorphosis at varying times. Yet, strand by strand, they each affect the look of your entire head of hair. God is so amazing! Not all of our hair falls out at one time (thankfully), and we only lose 50-125 strands a day. If you find yourself on the higher end of those numbers, don't panic. Factors such as your genetics, gender, age, hormones, and vitamin efficiency all have bearing on how much hair you will grow and keep. Don't hesitate to take time to consult with your stylist or a doctor (if necessary), if you find an excessive amount of shedding is happening.

Quick story-
One day, early in my cosmetology career (the 90's), I was doing my sister's hair at my very first salon in Richmond, California. Tracy had always had nice, fairly long, relaxed hair, and I was always trying something 'new' or 'hot' on her. (For the sake of the story, I need to give you the detail that my hair is a little rougher than my sister's. I could do everything to it, short of setting it on fire, and it would still be there. Standing tall…Thick as ever. I also had a relaxer at the time, and was fortunate enough to be able to color my hair as well as BLEACH a section of my "do" without any falling out. So, being a young stylist, I thought I could do the same to my sister. I didn't realize the difference in

hair texture was vital to the end results. Boy, this one was a tough lesson!)

I can't remember if my sister asked for colored hair or if I had suggested it. Nonetheless, I commenced to prep her, color her, and was looking forward to seeing the beautiful results of lightening her very dark hair to a light brown shade. Everything was going groovy until we got to that shampoo bowl…

As I turned on the nozzle, and began to thoroughly rinse the color from her hair, I noticed a bit of her hair washing into the bowl. But, I wasn't panicked. A little hair here or there - no problem I thought. I continued to rinse. Next thing you know, huge clumps of hair began to wash from her head right down the drain! I immediately felt hot from my head to my toes. The back of my neck felt like it could iron a shirt. I thought my heart was going to beat out of my chest! I got nauseous…I felt the walls closing in on me! I screamed, "Oh my GOD! Your hair is coming out!" I began to cry, being scared, sad, and embarrassed all at the same time. I couldn't believe that as much as I cared about my sister and her hair, I had caused such a disaster to happen. Surprisingly, my sister didn't seem to be very upset at all (either that or she's a HELL of an actress!). The bulk of her hair had fallen out on the left side/back of her head, and not a tear did she shed. I told her the only way we could make her hair look decent was to cut it. Even as I said it, I thought she would want to kill me. But, she was such a trooper. I'm still proud of her to this very day. Thank God for the asymmetric bob! I was able to cut her hair in a cute little brown style with one long side and the other side shaved down. She actually ended up loving it! So, the story didn't end so badly. But, the truth of the matter was this. I didn't have the full knowledge of how the chemicals I was using on my sister's hair were affecting her inner and outer layers. Consequently, my ignorance about the science of hair, led to me spending months upon months reconstructing, deep conditioning, moisturizing, treating, and loving her hair back to its glory. Despite the damage, I had done to the cuticle, cortex and medulla of her hair, the growth cycle allowed for her to eventually make a comeback. Thank heavens I was able to cut, style, and restore what she was left with, and I lived to tell the story. Stylists- I only ask that you invest in really knowing your stuff, when it comes down to color. Hair Enthusiasts- Please leave coloring your hair to the skilled professionals.

That day, I learned some very valuable lessons about hair and life:

1. MY SISTER _REALLY_ LOVES ME
2. YOU CANNOT TREAT EVERYONE'S HAIR THE SAME
3. LACK OF KNOWLEDGE CAN END IN TRAGEDY
4. YOU'RE ONLY AS GOOD OF A HAIRSTYLIST AS THE MISTAKES YOU CAN CORRECT

Hair Drawer Essentials

If you're like me, you have a hair product/tool cemetery someone in the bowels of your bathroom. It's probably under your sink or in a drawer where you can find batteries, lint rollers and pliers. This is the place where every product, clip, or curler that you've ever said 'yes' to (for one reason or another), has gone to die. The edge control that didn't hold your baby hairs down (like the girl in the beauty supply claimed), but instead had your hair frizzed up and cakey... Oh yes, the gel that flaked all over your cute, black, button up is there too. You know the one that had you looking like you needed to go home and shampoo your hair with some Head & Shoulders, even though you had just spent all day getting your hair together. I'm sure I don't need to go on... Here's the part of the Long Hair, Do Care where you get to rid your bathroom of all the stuff you've accumulated that really doesn't work. This is where you pick up the essentials every girl who truly wants long hair can't survive without.

Hair Drawer Necessities:

100% Silk Scarf: Not silk-y, silk-esque, or silk-ish, but 100% silk.

You can spend your money on something fancy or cute, if you'd like. But, for those who are minding their budgets, I suggest going to a fabric store and buying a yard of silk, or going to a vintage store and buying a scarf for a few dollars. You can wash it out with detergent or bleach (depending on the color) and it will dry within 30 minutes. ***This also applies to children.

Elastic Hair Bands (get rid of rubber bands and metal barrettes with sharp edges. Both of these products cut up your hair)

Butterfly hair clips (perfect for styling and
holding hair out of the way)

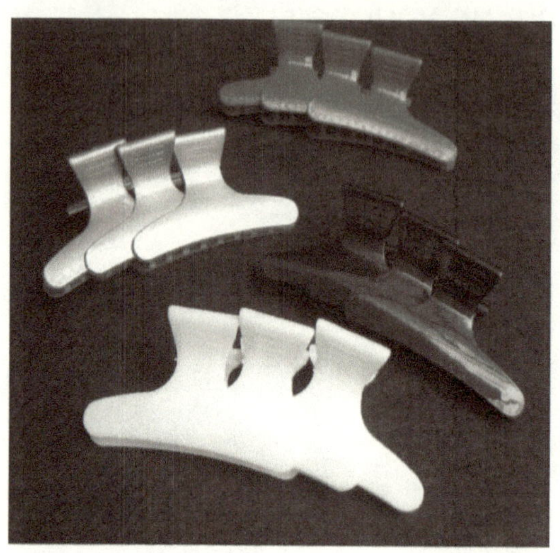

Duck bill hair clips

Hair pins and bobby pins

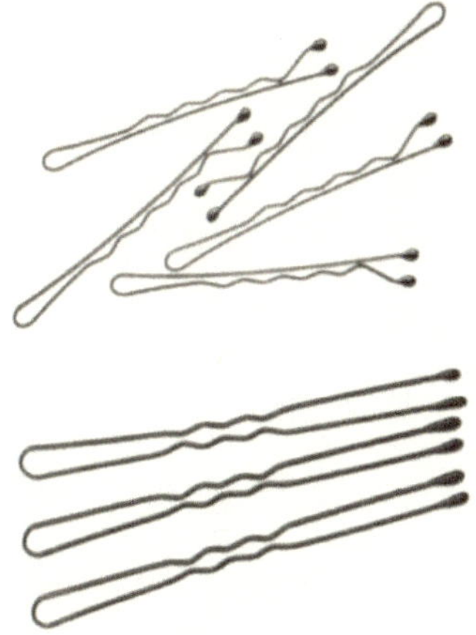

Hair gel

Edge control

Wide toothed comb

Rattail comb

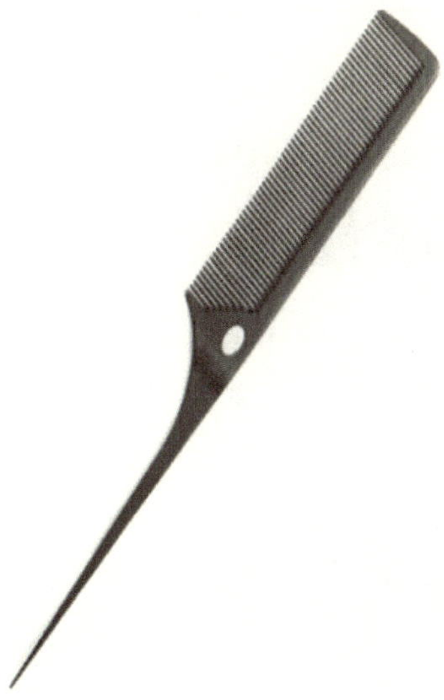

Detangled Brush by Felicia Leatherwood (my favorite)

Small wig brush or boar haired bristle brush

Shampoo & Conditioning

Shampooing:

When I was just a babe in hair school, one of my mentors, Betty Ferguson used say, "The shampoo bowl is where all of the magic happens". Truer words have never been spoken in Hairy Tale Land. The shampoo bowl is definitely the jumping off point for achieving long, healthy, hair. It's the place where all of the necessary additions and subtractions to the hair's bonds and the scalp take place. Equally as important, this is where the scalp gets clean as well. Both sebum and sweat combine on the scalp's surface and create an acid mantle, which is the skin's own protective layer. As the mantle increases, it shows up as flakes or greasy residue. In order for the hair and scalp to feel 'clean,' that layer has to be broken down and washed away, regularly. Here's how shampoo works: It breaks the surface tension of the water and allows the hair to become soaked (wet) and then cleaned. Each molecule of shampoo has both a head and tail on it. The head attracts water to the hair shaft, and the tail is attracted to grease, dirt, and oil. When all of the elements come together, grease and dirt are broken down and rinsed away.

Practically my entire career, I've found that most Black women feel the need to shampoo with harsh products in order to achieve a 'clean' head of hair. Many times, we want to use the 'extra strength' products to get that boost towards our desired results. Actually, nothing could be pushing you farther from your goals. Though our hair is tough, it is also fragile. Just like us. Because of this, I recommend you become an avid 'bottle reader.' There is some important information to be found. The main thing to look for is the pH of your shampoo and conditioner. pH is the 'potential of hydrogen,' meaning how alkaline or acidic a solution is on a scale from 0-14. What this means to you is your hair should be on the acidic side of the scale, which is less than 7. If it's on the higher side, your hair will look more dry and damaged. Your shampoo and conditioner bottles should say they have a pH no higher than 4-5.5. If the pH is not this low, then continue on. That product is too harsh for you, and is not going to give you the softness you seek. That low pH is going to keep the cuticle layer closed and maintain moisture, which is the secret sauce for SOFT, LONG, HEALTHY hair.

Shampoo Types

While there are many types of shampoos out there, I am going to recommend you use a moisturizing cleanser as your go-to (unless your hair is color treated). Because moisture is the most effective method for growing textured hair, I like to steer you towards products that build the hair and diminish the amount of water that can get in. Still, keeping in mind, there are various shampoos out there that will serve many purposes, but I will describe the functions of several products. When selecting a shampoo, I recommend a mid-range price point ($15 and up) and a brand that is NOT ethnicity specific for best results.

Moisturizing Shampoos restore moisture to the hair by way of humectants (moisture promoters), protein (hair bonds), and biotin (strengthener). They give elasticity (bounce back), strength and volume, but they don't strip or remove color from the hair. Using a moisturizing shampoo will keep your hair soft and manageable.

Clarifying Shampoos are good to use every 6-8 weeks as

they strip off pollutants, toxins, medications, wear and tear, silicone products, and a host of other chemicals that may be laying on the hair's surface. Make sure to deep condition after using this product, as it strips down the layers of your hair. ***A swimmer should use a clarifier once a week.

Color Enhancing (Pigmented) Shampoos work as normal shampoos do, but they have color molecules in them that they deposit color into the hair shaft. Those molecules, taken from plant extracts or dyes, latch into the cracks on the surface of the cuticle and fill them with a particular shade. It's really an awesome way to keep your color alive in between touch-ups. Whether you have black, brown, red, blonde, or grey hair, there is a shampoo AND conditioner out there that can help you to preserve your color. Depending on the manufacturer, you may get 2 or more weeks extra glow out of your hair color before it's time to pay the piper and come fresh again. Wearing gloves is a good idea to keep the color from staining your hands. Pigmented shampoos don't add aggressive color. Instead, they add a temporary tint that will eventually wear off or be shampooed from the hair.

Sulfate-Free Shampoos are quite mild and less harmful to the hair than normal shampoos because they don't contain harsh detergents. You'll know when a cleanser contains harsh sulfates, as it strips away natural oils and tends to be excessively foamy. Besides being gentler on the hair, another benefit of using a sulfate-free shampoo is that it preserves your hair color and protects it against the dulling that blow drying and over styling will do over time.

Medicated Shampoos are either over-the-counter or prescribed by a doctor or specialist to treat a particular problem with the scalp. Always consult a professional about what scalp condition you have and which product is best to use.

Soapless Shampoos have a pH of between 4 and 6 and contain no soap. They're more acidic than a normal shampoo and are closer to the pH of your natural hair. Acidic shampoos are most commonly used to maintain or improve the condition of the hair, because they don't swell the hair shaft or strip the natural oils.

Cleansing Conditioners also known as 'co-washing,' are just what they sound like: Conditioners that have cleansing properties. Because they are gentle, detergent-free, and have little to no sulfates, they don't do any lathering. But, they still manage to pull impurities out of the hair without leaving a heavy build-up. The true beauty of a cleansing conditioner is that it doesn't strip the hair its natural goodness. They contain essential oils that have cleansing properties. I love the cleansing conditioner option! If your hair has been chemically processed in any way, is extremely dry, or has really been damaged, this is a nice option in your shampooing regimen. However, it should not be used all the time.

The Godfather of Co-Washing-

Due to my love for all things 'the best,' and because I am completely biased towards the owner of the company, I will specifically mention the WEN cleansing conditioning products. I have had the pleasure not only to use this product, but also the honor to work very closely on a few projects with the creator/powerhouse Chaz Dean in the past (such a sweet guy and humble guy). Not only has he put me on some amazing shows and events, he was the first person that I ever saw using a conditioner to cleanse hair… like eons ago. It's popularly known as co-washing, now. I don't know if he has a title, but I'm going to name Chaz the 'Godfather of Co-Washing'. He was way ahead of the curve on that one. AND, he created his own product to boot! For straight or curly hair, co-washing will work very well. For naturally, kinky-curly hair, it is a great practice to integrate into your rotation. Whenever I want to go mild on my hair, I co-wash to break from the norm. On the times that I want to completely strip my hair down of all residues and build-up that may be on the surface, I revert back to my clarifying shampoo. The mix up allows my hair to be responsive to building it up from the inside out.

**FYI- Always read your bottles to be sure that your cleansing conditioners don't contain sulfates, soaps, parabens, or silicones.*

Conditioning

The job of a good conditioner is to repair the hair, both inside and out. They should always be used after shampooing to smooth down the cuticle layer of the hair, which can become roughened during the cleansing process. When hair begins to look frizzy or limp, it means the cuticle layer is being worn down, or has been weakened over time, and the overlapping cells are no longer lying snugly flat. It can also mean the cuticle layer has become loose, snagging against other strands, which causes them to tangle and sometimes break off. Either way, conditioners serve as an extra layer of protection against environmental damage. They contain high amounts of humectants and proteins which change the texture and appearance of hair, even after the conditioner is rinsed out.

There are three main types of conditioners that are normally combined:

1. Anti-oxidant Conditioners- mainly used in salons, mellow out the effects of chemical services and to slow down color fading.

2. Internal Conditioners- enter into the cortex and do the inside-work to keep the hair healthy (also known as treatments and masques).

3. External Conditioners- your everyday conditioners that smooth down the cuticle layer, making the hair shiny, easy to detangle, and smooth.

Here is a list of the different types of conditioners and how they work. Please consult your professional stylist to help you to decide what types of products will get you the results you need:

Protein or Reconstructive Conditioners- Hair is made up of about 97% keratin. Because we are constantly attacking it with a barrage of products, wear-and-tear, and heat, the cuticle will have chunks missing from it. These missing chunks make the hair more likely to split and break. So, it is mandatory in your hair schedule to regularly reconstruct. We have to trick the hair shaft into feeling like it is healed and all better, due to us constantly beating it up. Protein or the Reconstructor's role is to penetrate the hair and strengthen its structure through rebuilding (reconstructing) the bonds. It increases the diameter of the hair (making the surface appear to be thicker), the elasticity, and it equalizes porosity. The protein in these specific conditioners bond to the keratin layer of the hair, making it stronger, and recreating the broken surface layer.

Deep Conditioners/Masques- contain both protein and moisturizing properties. The humectants form bonds with the water from the air to seal moisture in the inner (cortex) layer of the hair. Those bonds reflect light, which makes the hair appear shiny. The beauty of a deep conditioner is it smooths down the cuticle and coats the shaft. When combined with heat, deep conditioners last longer than the norm and penetrate deeper, working on the hair from the inside and out.

Color Treated Hair Conditioners- contain no alcohols, peroxide, or ammonias to damage your hair. These conditioners deposit dye into the shaft, making it soft, and extending the life of the color. Trust me, there's nothing more disappointing than having a new hair color to play with and it fades quickly, because you used products that were too harsh. Color conditioners were made to either replace what is washed out in the shampooing process, or to accompany a color-enhancing shampoo. When you see words like "UVA/UVB protection on the bottle, that's code for 'protect and prevent' the sun from fading your precious color. Always follow the directions on the bottle. People with light colored hair must seek professional advice on which pigmented conditioners and shampoos will work best for their hair. *** *BEWARE- Color conditioner can make your hair feel coated after repeated use. It can have a semi-permanent effect and may not completely wash out of the hair.*

P.S. -Shampooing less frequently helps to preserve color.

Leave-In Conditioners

No matter what anyone says, never skip or consider

yourself done with your shampoo and conditioning routine without applying a leave-in conditioner. They are designed to prevent tangling and to keep the hair smoothed out. For those of us with naturally curly or kinky hair, leave-in conditioner should specifically be a cream (extra humectants) as opposed to liquid. Where the variety comes in is choosing if you want one for dry, damaged, color treated or one of the numerous other choices out there. The bottom line is- NEVER SHAMPOO AND CONDITION WITHOUT IT.

How to Shampoo and Condition Your Hair:

***Always comb through hair, removing tangles and knots before shampooing.

If your hair is super thick, long, or difficult to manage, shampooing your hair in plaited (braided) sections is a really good alternative to doing it while it's fully down. Just make sure you use enough product to penetrate the braid.

1.   Put a handful of shampoo in your hands

2.   Use both hands to split hair down the middle.

3.   Use the right hand to spread shampoo onto the scalp and hair.

4.   Split the left side of the half of hair in half with both hands and use the left hand to spread the shampoo on both sections of the hair.

5.   If necessary, apply more shampoo.

6.   Split the right side of hair in half with both hands.

7.   Use one hand to spread the shampoo on to both sections of your scalp and hair.

8.   Spread the remaining shampoo around your
        hairline, making sure to have thorough, all-over
        coverage (remember the center area).

9.   Agitate the shampoo at your scalp, with your
        fingertips or nails, for about 1 ½ minutes. Focus on
        the roots and not the ends, as doing the opposite
        causes tangling and split ends.

10.   Be sure to run the shampoo down your hair shaft.
        You may need to squeeze more shampoo into your
        hands. But, not necessarily.

11.   Rinse and repeat.

12.   Condition (follow the directions on the bottle).

13.   Comb through while conditioner is still on. If
        necessary, part hair into sections for more
        coverage and control.

14.   Rinse.

15.   Wring and towel dry.

16.   Apply leave-in conditioner and oil.

*If you find you are following all of the necessary
guidelines and your hair isn't responding the way you
believe it should, you may live in an area where the water
is laced with heavy mineral content, arsenic, fluoride, or is
heavily chlorinated. If you feel this is the case, it is
recommended that you use a filter in your shower and for
your drinking water*

Hair Oils

Ah, beloved hair oil! I can't stress enough how important it is in the journey to long, healthy hair. Ask anyone whose hair I have ever done. I'll bet you green money that they tell you I recommended them to use some type of hair oil on their hair at home. Oil absolutely *has* to be a part of your hair regimen. Not grease… Just oil. It keeps your hair soft, moisturized, and it prevents breakage. Many people mistakenly use grease to add moisture to their hair. *No way Jose'!* Grease <u>only</u> lies on the outside of your hair. It gives no benefit to the inner structure. Think of it like a slick, shiny blanket. The product that gives the most benefit is one that penetrates the cuticle and does the inside work. That is oil. There are various opinions about which oil is best. I always encourage people to experiment and go with what works best for their hair type. Also, mixing oils is totally awesome! Use one, or create your own concoction to use as you please. If you choose to buy oil off of the shelf, make sure it contains some of the ingredients listed here. If you're reading your label (I know you are, because you're an avid bottle reader) and see a bunch of chemicals you can't pronounce in the ingredients, that's a sign you should skip over this product.

****All ingredient lists start off with the products that are predominant at the top. That's true for any products that you purchase.*

If you have thick hair, you can use a variety of different oils (especially if your hair is natural). Coconut oil, Olive oil, Jojoba oil, Vitamin E oil, Safflower oil, Sweet Almond oil, Castor oil, Sesame oil, Wheat Germ oil, There is no one specific type that is necessary to use.

If your hair is on the thicker side, and you are chemically straightening, an occasional 1-2 drops (a dime size) of oil before you blow dry or tie your hair up at night will add a light, natural luster to your hair.

For clients with thinner hair that is chemically treated, I recommend a very light portion (one drop) of Vitamin E oil, Sweet Almond oil, or Coconut oil. If you have natural hair you can use more to help with creating your styles. If you are straightening your hair, stay with to 1 drop of oil. If your hair is curly and you want to rock a natural look (even though your hair will absorb moisture more quickly), be mindful of how much oil you're applying, because you don't want to give yourself the Jheri (what does cheri mean?) curl effect.

Blow Dry 101

****This chapter is not focused on natural hair drying, when it is to be worn in its kinky state. Those styles generally require sitting under a hooded dryer to achieve a desired look. But, the key to a successful natural do, is to make sure the hair is completely dry to consider the style complete****

Haven't you seen that woman with a shiny, bouncy, glow to her hair? It looks like the sun, stars, and all of the lights in the universe are shooting rays right to her head! You know the glow that no matter what combination of products you use, it eludes you? Part of the issue is the glow doesn't necessarily come from products. But, the other part could be that you haven't yet gotten to the "kwan" (aka money spot) of blow drying just yet. But, I'm here to help you to become that glowing ray of light you're meant to be. Following the steps below can lead to YOU being the woman with the hair everyone wants. A huge part of getting the bounce, luster, and shine is properly manipulating the salt bonds with your blow dryer (Oh yes, hair contains salt too!). Now that you've gotten through the shampoo and conditioning steps of our hair ritual, it's time to dry your hair like a BOSS.

There are two weapons you cannot live without in your hair care arsenal. 1) A BOMB blow dryer and 2) A hooded (sit under) dryer. Let no one tell you that you don't need both. Buying the right hand held hairdryer can actually save you up to 30 minutes off of your beautification process. I recommend purchasing one that is at least 1875 watts. Ionic, Tourmaline and Ceramic dryers are all great choices.

****Remember**: *Heat + Product makes the salt bonds in your hair illuminate!*

Tools You Will Need:

Leave-in conditioner

Oil

Wide toothed comb

Paddle brush

Clips

If you ask 10 different hairstylists what steps they take to dry their clients hair, you'll get 10 different answers. There are millions of methods to use, in accordance to what suits your needs and resources. As for me, I always pick the fastest, most-effective, and healthiest means that I know to get to an end (no matter what I'm doing to the hair). I developed this habit because I've probably clocked 9 million salon hours from childhood until now. I'm always eager to get my work done, because I love play time! Plus, the only thing worse than having an impatient client looking upside your face, because they've been in the shop for too long, is dredging out the styling process, and having your client looking upside your face while you're working hard to end it all and get paid. I've learned, the hard way to maximize my time. I do this, by knowing how long it takes me to do every operation I perform. I figured out how to schedule myself to get people in and out of my chair. Time management equals appreciation, which quickly turns into dollars. Even though you may not be a professional, using this information on yourself, your friends, or your children will save you time and energy. That being said, on a daily basis, I use one of two methods to get my clients hair dry quickly and healthily as possible:

The Hooded Dryer Method & The Handheld Blow dry Method

*** These steps should be followed after you have applied a quarter sized squirt of leave-in conditioner and a dime size portion of hair oil (depending on your length and thickness) to your hair.***

Hooded Drying

When it comes down to a hooded dryer, not only will it help to dry your hair in a laid back style, but it will be a life saver in the deep conditioning, masque, and treatment phase of your hair care regimen. Many people don't realize that when hair is wet, it is at its weakest state. How many days have we sat through the blow dry comb pulling and raking through our hair until it dries? PAIN AND AGONY... not to mention HARD WORK! I really don't recommend using this method, because it usually doesn't aid in growing long, healthy hair. Raking and pulling doesn't promote the smoothness of the hair cuticle (top layer). I mean, you do have a chance for success, but, there is also a great possibility for breakage and split ends. I don't ever want you to run that risk. AND- I'm going to always do the thing that gets you that shiny, bouncy, healthy hair you desire.

Here are the hooded drying steps I use on myself and my clients:

1. Comb the hair into four sections.

2. Plait the sections into four loose braids

3. Sit under the dryer for about 20-30 minutes (sometimes the hair will not be completely dry and that's okay).

4. Come out from under the dryer and use your handheld to dry your hair completely (from ends to roots), using a paddle brush (it usually takes about 10 minutes of 'brush blow drying' to get to the desired straightness).

5. Style as necessary.

(If appropriate)In the case that your hair is relaxed, mold your hair into the desired style, and sit under the dryer until you have reached complete dryness. When you come from under the dryer, blow dry (on normal heat) using your handheld dryer, to achieve further straightening, body, and shine.

Handheld Blow drying

The second drying technique involves using your handheld blow dryer. I tend to use this method when I either, 1) don't have access to a hooded dryer, or I'm 2) trying to complete a style in a short amount of time (if you have the time, I recommend you use the first method). Handheld blow drying alone can be just as damage free as the first method, if done using the right amount of care. I've used this method for many years too, and have had much success with achieving long, healthy hair with my clients.

Here are my steps for handheld blow drying:

1. Air-dry the hair (finger comb the hair from root to ends as you pull it straight, running the dryer up and down the hair shaft). This is the substitution for going under the dryer.

2. Part your hair into four sections.

3. Comb each section out from the ends to the roots and braid it.

4. Starting with a back section, unbraid and pull through it with your fingers, then comb all tangles out.

5. Hold the bottom of the entire section and pull it as straight and taught as you can.

6. Turn on your blow dryer to its regular heat setting (professionals can use high heat) and starting from the roots to the ends, pass the blow dryer (with little to no space between the dryer and your hair) up and down the hair shaft quickly without stopping. As you do this, you will see smoke and feel the heat very close to your scalp. All of this is normal. Repeat this action to the top, bottom, and sides of the section until it's 90% (very close to being) dry.

7. Grab your wide-toothed comb and comb through the section, from the ends to the roots, to remove the tangles that will gather (especially on the ends).

8. (This step can be done two ways)Grab your paddle brush and blow dry, slowly, from ends to root with the brush method. Or, get your pick attachment (which I, personally, never use) and begin to, slowly, blow dry from the ends to the roots.

9. Repeat in the remaining 3 sections.

10. Once each section is completely dry, go remove the pick attachment and air dry the roots of your hair for about 30 seconds.

*** It is important to go back through your hair and remove* *the parted sections you have created during the blow dry process. Failing to do so will lead to permanent section divisions in your hairstyle. So, be sure, when using your pick attachment, to either comb the parts out, or to part the hair off in the way you want the finished style to look when your hairstyle is completely done.****

Trimming

This will, undoubtedly, be a short section (no pun intended!). I know it seems funny that in a book about growing long hair we'd be talking about pulling out scissors, but it's a very necessary part of maintaining length and health of your hair. My first rule of thumb concerning anything having to do with taking scissors to hair is: **Leave it to the professionals**. I cannot tell you how many hair massacres I've had to fix. Sometimes we have the grand idea that we can do more to our hair than is realistic. The main issue is, even if we can get by with making the front of our hair look decent ourselves- We can't see the back of our own heads! Even in the case that we can see it, 9 times out of 10 we don't have the acrobatic skills to reach all of the sections that need attention. Nonetheless, it's important to know one thing: serious length can't be achieved with raggedy ends. If your hair is damaged, it is better to cut the damage off than to try to manage dry, long, split, ends. You can have your stylist do the 'big chop,' if you're feeling brave. Or, you can have her/him take off your damaged ends little by little (a 1/4" at a time), if a drastic change doesn't suit you. On an average, one should trim her/his ends every 6-8 weeks. However, there is always the exception to the rule. If you've mastered your hair routine, there is the possibility you can go about 2-3 months before they need to trim. When you don't trim your hair and it already has split ends, they just continue to split higher and higher up the hair shaft. Split ends can go all the way up to the roots and become split hairs. Imagine your hair being a rope that has begun to unravel. If left undone, it will just continue to unravel all the way up to the top until it's no good.

The 'WHAT's & 'WHY's of Protective Styles

A protective hair style is one that is solely done for the purpose of keeping your hair completely covered and safe from damage. The base of most protective styles (even extensions) consists of some type of braids, twists, or up dos. These styles shield your hair as it grows, so that when you take them down, you will have grown as much damage-free hair as is possible.

Protective styles are awesome! Why? Because they allow for a break from combing and brushing. Both can lead to breakage, shedding and damage (Remember, the #1 rule of long, healthy, hair is to do as little to it as possible). By giving the hair time to rest (not combing daily), we allow the hair that has grown out at the roots to be added to the hair that has been wonderfully maintained on the ends.

A protective style should be left up for no more than 8 weeks. I know there are ladies out there who are running the braid and weave marathon. But, I'm telling you- You are doing yourself more harm than good. In the long run, you will lose way more hair than you gain. By the time you comb out all of the dreadlocks and tangles you've accumulated from repeatedly shampooing and conditioning (or not), you are going to have a hair ball of epic proportions to deal with. It's better to just take down your hair, pause, and wear your hair for a week or two in between. Then do it all over again, after your hair has rested. That's the way to win with a protective style.

There is a serious warning that goes along with protective

dos:

Be very cautious of how tightly your stylist pulls your ponytail, your braids, or twists your hair, especially when it comes to your edges and thin areas.

First things first- No tight braids on edges EVERRRRR!!! Too much stress on the fine hairs around one's hairline or thin spots can result in temporary (and sometimes permanent) damage. When the hair is pulled too tightly away from the scalp, the bulbs of the hair give way, creating thinness or even balding. If you ever notice those tiny white dots attached to a full strand of hair, when it's pulled very tightly, you have just witnessed root damage in the first degree. That tiny white speck is the bulb of your hair. It can regenerate. But, in the case of being repeatedly snatched out, or where years of abuse and tension have occurred, women have been known to suffer from permanent baldness Trust me, I've seen it countless times with braids, extensions, locks, twists, and ponytails. Stylists are often heavy handed when it comes to the sensitive parts of a client's head. It is absolutely not necessary to be rough around your client's edges. And let's be real- having sensitivity to a client's needs is a huge part of doing hair.

Story break-

A common belief, held by many people, is that leaving your hair under a protective style, time after time, is healthy. I found out the hard way, that hair needs to be exposed to the elements, to grow properly. What makes it worse is I learned my lesson on a long time client of mine. A very nice and loyal client, she had fragile hair (early onset of female patterned baldness) when we met. Not super damaged...just fragile. At first we were doing her own hair, and we got great results from treating her on a regular basis. But then we started doing extensions on her... for at least a full year! Without going into all of the gory details of the situation, I will say I knew that repeatedly putting extensions in her hair was not the best idea, especially, considering her texture. However, I kept putting the extensions in, because it worked well for both of us. She had a full beautiful hairstyle, and I had a consistent, well-paying, client. Well, long story short, after repeatedly putting extensions in her hair time after time, with no rest periods in between, my client ended up pissed because one day when we removed the extensions, she had noticeably thinner hair. It actually shocked the both of us! For her, the shock was not realizing what shape her hair had been in. For me, it was seeing how a situation I thought I had under control got away from me (remember, she had the onset of female patterned baldness when she got on the extensions train). By the time I took the extensions out for the last time, there was a minor cowlick situation going on. Of course, our professional relationship ended. It made me very sad because I ended up with a mark on my professional reputation AND my conscience. I also lost a very sweet, kind, and loyal customer. I felt like a complete ASS! I didn't do what I KNEW was right, and it ended up costing me on many levels.

Moral of the story- *Learn from my mistake. Always do the right thing...Especially, when it comes to hair.*

Can You Stand the Heat?

(How much is too much?)

We already know that hair is made up of protein, water, keratin, salt, as well as an array of other scientific stuff. So, let's talk about a few ways heat affects all of that stuff. Because it breaks down and re-forms the structure of the hair's bonds, heat can be used for either awesomeness or for terribleness (are those words?). If applied properly (with deep conditioning treatments), heat can help to keep the cuticle layer close snugly around the inner workings of the hair shaft (which is a good thing). When carefully used, heat can straighten the hair and alter its texture… (sometimes permanently, if overly done). I don't know if you've ever heard of the term 'pocket curls.' But, if you haven't, let me get you up to speed. Pocket curls is a term stylists use when she/he is curling you up (usually with marcel irons) and accidentally puts too much heat on your hair- to the degree where the curl gets burned off. And, of course to cover up the fact that your hair is gone (because who signs up for that?), your stylist just takes the hair and puts it in her/his pocket for safe keeping (as to not piss you off). Foul, right? I knoooow! Later on, when you discover the space in your hair, the stylist can claim that she/he doesn't know how you got it, or who is responsible. It's a real cloak and dagger maneuver. But, I promise you that any stylist, worth a hill of beans that has worked with marcel irons has done it. I have to admit that I've pulled it a time or two, in my career (especially when freeze curls were in style). But, I digress… The point is, that some long term damage that can take anywhere from months to years for your hair to recover from can happen from the misuse of heat. Although it does take just the right amount of heat to achieve a good hairstyle, I will always recommend going to a professional for that initial high powered styling. Maintaining whatever work your stylist does, with your heat tools at home, is fine. I do recommend that you not 'go crazy' with the heat. Blow dryers, flat irons, pressing combs and curling irons have taken down a many of good intentioned at home hairdressers. The one rule of thumb I ask my clients to follow is to NOT get your flat irons or curling irons smoking hot when you're doing your maintenance. It's actually overkill (especially if you have chemically treated hair). I would not recommend getting flat irons or curlers that exceed a temperature more than 430 degrees for at home use. The main thing to do is to get a properly shaped hairstyle that's easy to maintain, tie it up every night (and, I mean religiously!), wake up, spray on some shine, and do as little to maintain your look as possible during the course of the day. I can't stress this enough - leaving your hair alone and allowing it to grow with very little interference, is the best way to get to long, healthy hair. Think of people with locks or braids. Their hair gives the illusion that it grows faster. But, really the hair is growing at the same rate as everybody else's; it's just that it's not being tampered with every day. So, it seems like it's growing super-fast! The reality is that it's just not being pulled out.

The key to working heat into your routine is to make sure that you give your hair the proper care so that it can recover. That takes us back to the area where the magic happens- The shampoo bowl. Through moisturizing and reconstructing with shampoos and conditioners, you are restoring the water and proteins, as well as sealing breakage that comes along with turning up the heat. So, keep it healthy loves!

My Chemical Romance/Transitioning to Natural Hair

Natural hair is AMAZEBALLS! I've pretty much worn my hair in its natural state for the past 15 years (minus the first year that I moved to Atlanta and I thought it would be a good idea to relax my hair instead of fighting it out with the humidity... WRONG!!!). It was an amazing transition for me, because I had worn a relaxer for about 1000 years. When I made my decision, I was a little fearful, because I hadn't dealt with my real hair texture since I was 12 years old. I was so scared because I had always been told my hair was 'SO thick' and so hard to handle. Length was never my strong suit. I just accepted that I had this 'bad', nappy, thick, hair that everyone had trouble whipping into shape. But, I had made a commitment to brave it out. I was going all the way, and I knew I didn't want to cut all of my hair off and start from scratch. I decided that doing lock extensions was the answer. I had seen both Lauren Hill and Erykah Badu do them with much success, so I felt confident in my choice. I always wanted dreadlocks since I was a young child, but my Dad told me there was no way he was letting me put "those funky things" in my hair". He was convinced (by the homeless people that he'd seen wearing them on the street of San Francisco) that the hairstyle was the result of bad hygiene, and there was no way he was giving me a vote for that! So, at 30 years old, I finally got my chance to do the style I had been wanting since I was about a child. I was going to have my locks!

Initially, I did not cut off my relaxer. I had been rocking a short little 'fly girl' haircut for years, and had let it grow out for a couple of months, so that I could begin to flat iron it. As time passed, and I became more familiar with my hair, I discovered that my natural hair wasn't hard to deal with at all! Here are some other things I came to know: 1. My Mom (as sweet as she is) was just a little challenged with the hair styling (Plus, my hair was no cakewalk when I was younger). And 2. My Dad, who owned a salon and was a hairstylist, really only began doing my hair when he gave me my first relaxer at 12 years of age. He used to try to give me the Claire Huxtable roller sets in elementary school. I COULD. NOT. DEAL. My real problem was that I had just been out in the natural hair wilderness for the early part of my life. In reality, my hair was neither too 'bad' nor too thick, it was just unfamiliar territory.

This is the place where I need to break and talk about the history of perpetual self-hate that has attached itself to Black women, through our hair texture.

I briefly talked about being a little girl with a 'nappy kitchen' and just medium length hair, at best. Thank God, I had a little personality. I could get by with jokes and a sense of humor to make up for whatever I was 'lacking' in the hair department, by society's standards. I was just trying to find some kind of way to fit in with everyone else. A girl never forgets the insecurity of feeling that she's not quite enough. Those scars run deep. I'd be lying if I said that I haven't seen grown women who are still nursing the wounds that they accumulated from the cruelty they experienced at the hands of their peers for being 'bald headed' or 'nappy headed' or for not having 'good hair'. Even today, we witness those scars exist. Big dollars are being spent at the beauty supply stores and with independent sellers on hair extensions and relaxers. Don't get me wrong, styling your hair how you want is no crime. But, all of the poisonous, residual self-hatred imposed on people of color by our captures (slave masters) has to be recognized and destroyed. It's time to embrace the beauty of who we are on the inside, whether natural, chemically treated, or bald for that matter. This hair is just a piece of our outer shell. As long as your hair is clean, healthy, and well styled, it's all lovely. If it grows out of your scalp, it's good. Everything else can be worked out. I won't stay on my soapbox right now. I realize that I can't undo all of the damage that we have inflicted on each other with our antiquated thoughts. I would; however, like to encourage people of color to stop judging one another by the texture and length of our hair (not to mention skin tone). It's super wack.

Now, back to our regularly scheduled programming...

I was working at Millennium Salon in Los Angeles at the time of my 'let's go back to natural' metamorphosis, and there were a number of amazing hair wizards working there with me. One of them was my girl Felicia Leatherwood. I would watch her work her natural hair magic on clients day after day… over and over again. After having seen her do some natural twist extensions on a client one day, I decided I knew what I was doing well enough to try my hand at some do-it-yourself locks. I had grown my hair out about four inches, by that time, and had begun to be very used to my texture. Once I got those locks in, baby that was it! I didn't look back for seven whole years. Even after that time, I continued to wear my hair natural, because I had gotten used to the richness of my texture. I absolutely loved my nappy hair (not to diss my relaxed hair, because it was great too. I just prefer a chemical-free life)! Over the years, I learned to embrace the routine of moisturizing, conditioning, protecting, and

I wanted to share my natural hair story with you, so you could know just how much I loved my journey. But, I cannot discount all of those years prior to me having a relaxer, because I equally enjoyed that experience. In both cases, my hair was always healthy *and cute* (LOL!). Realize that just because my natural hair story worked out for me, it doesn't mean that yours will for you. Not every natural hair journey will be a love affair. If you find yourself trying to manage your chemical free tresses and it's turning out NOT to be your cup of tea, you have to do what makes you comfortable. Sure, I hate to think of you frying your brain with all the chemicals in a straightener. But, I ain't mad at you for doing what you have to do to maintain your look...Because nothing is worse than a raggedy head! We (the naturalistas) still love and accept you. Listen, I have run the full gamut of hairstyles as well as given them out. I can truly say natural hair is an acquired taste. Sometimes, when we take a position to join 'team natural' or 'team relaxer,' we have a tendency to become judgmental of the other side. Both teams can find reasons why the other's choice is not the way. I won't take sides, but here's what I will say: Hair, in its natural state, is very strong, and it is less likely to break. Other than the fact it requires *more* product to keep it healthy and moisturized, you essentially use the same products on it as when your hair is chemically treated. But the bottom line is, whichever route you choose it's always best to see your stylist and keep your hair healthy as possible.

Hair Vitamins (The ABC's of A, B, D, & E)

Many times when we think about growing long healthy hair, we have a tendency to forget that it is a full body process. Proper nutrition is a key element in the foundation for optimal hair health. You're the full package, honey. So, full wellness must be a regular part of your life! When we take care of ourselves all around, we see the results. In earlier chapters, I mentioned that the living part of the hair is housed in the follicle, under the scalp skin, where the root is located. The entire root and follicle are fed by a vein that carries its nutrients. Therefore, it's super important to eat healthy, non-gmo, wild, organic foods, whenever possible, as to carry nutrients to your scalp. In the best case scenario, you would bombard your body with goodies that are high in vitamins A (produces oil), the B family, D (helps to create and awaken new follicles), E (helps to repair damage done to the tissue and follicles, encouraging growth), folic acid (keeps the blood flowing properly), omega 3s (adds hydration), and especially biotin (the protein makeup of the hair). You can also opt to take those same vitamin supplements. All of these vitamins add to the balanced array of nutrients in the recipe for long hair, as well. Vitamin B-5 (pantothenic acid) gives hair flexibility, strength, shine, and helps to prevent hair loss and graying. Vitamin B-6 helps prevent dandruff, and vitamin B-12 helps prevent hair loss. Out of all of the vitamins listed, **biotin** is most important, in regards to hair, because it is the vital part of the keratin, enzyme, and amino acid makeup of the fiber.

By listing these hair boosting super vitamins, I'm hoping for a scenario where you eat all of the food that gives you the amazing hair that you dream of. To make 'hair growing foods' easy to recognize, I have created a list of yummy stuff that you can add to your diet to give you that good-good hair. If you find it hard to eat your vitamin intake, I recommend taking supplements. If you decide that that's what works for you, my first suggestion is to use only 100% natural vitamin products free of hormones, dairy, and preservatives. I ask that you become an avid reader of the labels of the foods, drinks, vitamins, and anything else that you put into or on your precious body. When browsing hair vitamin bottles, the key ingredients that you want to keep your eye out for are biotin (most important), alpha lipoic acid (second most important), b complex, omega 3, collagen, and folic acid. **Remember: Good nutrition in = good hair out**.

BEWARE!

Many advertisers will make claims for this or that vitamin brand, but if you're perusing a bottle and you don't see the ingredients that I've named above, drop that puppy right back on the shelf (or leave it on that pretty little website), and head for the hills.
Men lie, women lie, numbers and (most) ingredients don't.

Long Hair, Do Care Hair Food List

Important! Please Read: Please do not substitute the information given on vitamin intake for a doctor's advice. Do not take these vitamins if you are currently pregnant or planning to become pregnant. Studies have shown that a high intake of vitamin A is known to contribute to birth defects. Collagen is a known animal protein derivative. If you are vegan, vegetarian or are

abstaining from meat for any reason, collagen may not be for you. When consuming high volumes of vitamin B, it is suggested that one consume an increased amount of water. If you have issues with your kidneys or are on a low protein diet, consult your physician before taking any forms of hair, nail and skin enhancing vitamins.

Vitamin A: sweet potatoes, carrots, dark leafy greens, winter squash, lettuce, apricots, cantaloupe, bell peppers, fish, liver, tropical fruits.

Vitamin D: cod liver oil, mushrooms, oily fish, whole grain cereals, tofu, lean meats, eggs, soy/almond/cashew/rice milk.

Vitamin E: dark leafy greens, nuts (almonds, pistachios, pecans, walnuts), seeds(sunflower seeds, pumpkin, squash, sesame), avocados, shellfish (oysters, shrimp, crawfish), fish (salmon, rainbow trout, swordfish, herring), plant oils (olive, sunflower, grapeseed, wheat germ), broccoli, squash & pumpkin, fruits (kiwi, blackberries, mangos, peaches, nectarines, apricots, mulberries, guavas, raspberries).

Vitamin B-1: green peas, squash, asparagus, edamame, beans (navy, pink, black, mung).

Vitamin B-2: cheese (goat, feta, brie, parmesan, Roquefort, camembert), almonds, beef, lamb, oily fish (wild salmon, wild tuna, wild herring, wild trout), eggs, mushrooms, shellfish (oysters, clams, mussels), greens (beet greens, collards, dandelion, Chinese broccoli).

Vitamin B-3: fatty fish (mackerel, halibut), foul (chicken, turkey), beef, liver, peanuts.

Vitamin B-5: sweet potatoes or yams.

Vitamin B-6: pistachios, dried fruit (prunes, apricots, raisins), bananas.

Vitamin B-12: crab, tofu (soy products), bran cereals, whey protein, yogurt.

Folic Acid: beans, lentils, dark leafy greens, lettuce, broccoli, mangos, oranges.

Collagen: fish, red vegetables (beets, peppers, tomatoes), dark leafy greens, orange vegetables (carrots, peppers, sweet potatoes), berries, soy, white tea, citrus fruit, eggs, lean meats, peanuts, garlic.

Biotin: Mushrooms, tuna, turkey, avocados, Swiss chard, eggs, salmon, sunflower seeds, lover, peanut butter, cheese, cauliflower, whole grain bread, sardines, berries, almonds, bananas, soybeans.

Alpha Lipoic Acid: spinach, broccoli, tomato, green peas, Brussels sprouts, rice bran.

Omega 3s: flaxseed oil, fish oil, chia seeds, walnuts and walnut oil, caviar, smoked fish, shellfish (oysters, mussels, and clams), squid, soybeans, spinach.

Hair Loss and the State of You

When I came up with the idea to write a book on how to grow long hair, I wanted to create something that would not only help women to learn growing techniques, but one that would explain (in simple terms) the science and makeup of hair and how to keep it on their heads. I wanted to write something that would be useful to both the average woman, as well as the beauty professional. But, I knew I couldn't ignore the one topic that affects us all sooner or later- *hair loss*. Remember, there is a distinct difference between *shedding*, *breakage, and hair loss*.

- Shedding is at the root, and is part of a natural cycle. It's nature's way of saying 'out with the old and in with the new.'

- Breakage happens along the hair shaft and is usually the result of chemical damage and plain old abuse.

- Hair loss is caused by an internal imbalance (which is quite serious).

Although Long Hair, Do Care has addressed how to stop hair breakage in previous chapters, we're going to get more into the internal works of your hair and body, so that you can get a better understanding of how to keep your tresses in optimal shape. In this section, we're going to talk about some factors that can lead to hair loss, when it's time to see a doctor, and various ways to bounce back from heavy medication.

Factors that Lead to Hair Loss

Any time a person has any kind of health concerns, her/his hair will be affected. Factors such as stress, trauma, medications of various sorts, chronic medical conditions and ones that come and go, hormonal issues, heavy metals in waters/foods, or smoking and the like, take a tremendous toll on the hair. All of these factors put a strain on its growth and appearance. A mild case of anemiacan cause a great deal of shedding. Fluctuations in hormones will often show up in the hair. Sometimes those changes are minor and can be easily alleviated with diet, exercise, and vitamins. But more severe cases may call for the help of a doctor and/or an herbalist, and can often take months for consistent results to show up. Depending on what phase of the growth cycle your hair is in, treatment for a hormonal condition may seem to be at a standstill, or even to revert at a certain point. Also, hereditary factors must be considered when dealing with hair loss. Male and female pattern baldness can both come into play, when considering why one is being plagued by this condition.

If you notice that your hair is coming out in clumps, it may be a sign of a thyroid condition. The first sign of thyroid issues usually shows up in the behavior of the hair. Women are the most under-diagnosed for thyroid disease. If you think that this may be of concern to you, ask your gynecologist about doing a blood screening exam on your next visit.

If you are pregnant and/or breast feeding, your normal shedding process will be on hold starting around the three month point. You will notice that your hair is thicker, shinier, has more body, or may even change colors while you're pregnant and breast feeding. Once you have the baby and your body gets back to its normal routine, you may have an excessive amount of shedding, because your body is playing catch up to get back to its normal routine. If this is happening to you, it will take 3-6 months before the shedding stops and your hair gets back to normal.

Factors that affect hair loss:

1. Your current state of health- Thyroid, chemotherapy, hormones, chronic illness, etc.

    a. Are you on medication?

    b. Do you get enough sun and exercise?

    c. Do you have sufficient nutrients in your system to maintain overall health?

    d. What is your stress level?

2. Are you stressing your hair?

    b. Do you tie your hair up too tight (or at all)?

    c. Are you pulling out your edges?

    d. Do you have chemical damage?

    e. Do you have a nervous habit of picking your hair?

4. What season of the year it is (Hair grows faster in the Spring and Summer).

When it's time to see the Doctor-

Your body will feel the distinctive differences between what's normal for you, and when it's time to see a doctor. At the point when you're noticing lasting scales, flakes, burning, pus or leakage from the scalp, it's time to see a dermatologist or Trichologist. Both specialize in treating disorders of the skin and scalp. Either can diagnose a condition and take all of the guess work out of what can be done in a particular case. Diseases like alopecia, rashes, hair pulling/picking, and chemical burns should always be addressed by a medical professional. Seek immediate professional help if you are experiencing any of the following symptoms:

Bald patches

Bleeding

Bumps

Clumps of hair falling out

Dandruff (cornflake-like scales and clumps that are resistant to lifting from the scalp)

Exceptionally Dry hair & scalp

Foul odor coming from your scalp

High volume shedding

Patches of extremely thin hair

Persistent itchiness (despite oil and shampooing)

Pus-like drainage

Rashes and discolored inflammation on the scalp

Redness/Scalp irritation

Bouncing Back from Heavy Medication

The first thing to realize about bringing your hair and body back from heavy doses of medication is that it will take time. Medication changes us- physiologically, mentally, and even spiritually. Medicine (drugs) may cause damage to the brain, destroying nerve cells and disrupting the neural circuitry (brainwaves). Drugs may affect your memory, eyesight, mood, sex-drive and cognitive functions. God is so perfect, in the way we are made. Everything (down to the cellular level) within us wants to be perfect and well. The body is such a forgiving machine. If we even remotely treat it right, it will perform magnificently for us. Cells can regenerate and our brain can be rewired in time, to perform as optimally as we are willing to nurture it back to health. The chemical break in your wiring, though sometimes necessary, must be given ample time to get back to normal. But, it can be done. The key to great health and recovery is what we put into ourselves, and what we do with our bodies. Please refer to (and follow) the food chart that was given in the **Hair Vitamins** chapter. I'm a living witness that all of the foods and vitamins can bring you back from even the brink of death, if you are consistent. Even though I've already mentioned most of the items on this list, I want to remind you of some of the 'must haves' for bouncing back from heavy medication:

- Take Omega 3s

- Get 8 hours of sleep a night

- Elevate your fatty acid and 'good fat' intake (nuts, flaxseed, avocado)

- Eat organic, chemical free, non-GMO foods

- NO PROCESSED FOODS! (That means no iodized salts, no bleached or processed sugar, flour, white rice, white bread and bleached pasta. No PRESERVATIVES. Healing requires at least 120 grams of carbohydrates per day. Stay away from saturated fats. No excess caffeine. No canned and rarely any jarred foods (you have to do some extreme label reading to find exceptions)

- Drink lots of water (adding chlorophyll helps)

- Fast and cleanse on a monthly basis

Major Key Alert: If you are trying to rid yourself of toxins, you can't live without:WHEATGRASS. **WHEATGRASS IS AMAZEBALLS!** In order for it to do magical things for you, you must drink it fresh. Beware! It tastes like falling face down on a football field on a rainy day. But, it is a super food (in my NOT medically certified opinion)! Why do I say such a thing? Well, I've taken wheatgrass for many years and it has brought me a long way. It has solved everything with me from fighting a cold to combatting my anemia. It actually contains vitamins A, B-Complex, C, E, I, and K. All of which were listed as essential for hair growth. It's also very high in protein and contains amino acids. Again, more elements that hair is actually made from. The biggest plus about wheatgrass is that it keeps you from getting old fast. You know we ladies love that (wink, wink)! The main ingredient of wheatgrass (chlorophyll) washes the remnants of drugs and heavy metals out of your system and cleanses your blood. So, when you're trying to recover from the poison and toxins that drugs put into your body, wheatgrass will get you right. Another benefit is that it is high in vitamin K, the secret weapon for fighting gray hair from forming. Can you believe it? The secret sauce to keeping you and your hair youthful.

GURU Loves the Kids

Children are the joys of our lives, and nothing makes us happier than to keep them safe, happy, and looking beautiful. So, I had to include a section for the little ones! If you've learned anything about me from reading this book, you know that I'm going to always try to give you a deeper understanding of what's at the core of the hair. I do this so that you can know WHY you're doing everything that you're doing. Of course, this section will be no exception. Believe it or not, mostly everything we've covered in *Long Hair, Do Care* also applies to children's hair. But, here are a few extras that we have to keep in mind when dealing with the kid's hair:

1.   A child's hair is in a very fragile state up until she/he is around seven years old.

2.   Your child's hair becomes semi-mature when she/he gets to be around twelve years old.

3.   Until the hair reaches its beginning stages of maturity, stay away from over cleansing, excessive heat, tight ponytails and braids, and chemical straighteners for as long as possible.

At the time of our birth, a baby has the most hair follicles that they will have in life. As she/he matures, she/he will lose hair. In actuality, if properly cared for, a person's hair is in its greatest condition in our earliest years. During childhood the medulla is missing from the center of the hair shaft, causing it to be fine and soft. This is really the reason that care is so critical. Children also have less melanin (color) in their hair. Take a look at some of your old baby pictures. Some of you may have been blonde or had very light hair. As an adult, you now have darker colored hair. That means that medulla is now developed. So, when you notice that your child's hair color getting darker, that's a sure sign that the hair is maturing.

Here are some steps you can take to keep your little one's hair healthy:

1. Always lightly spray your child's hair down with a mixture of lotion-y leave-in oil mixed with water (making it thoroughly damp) before you comb it out. Always go from ends to roots, with a wide toothed comb, before styling or shampooing.

2. Always shampoo and condition with a natural (no parabens, sulfates, phosphates, artificial colors, or artificial fragrances. It should also have a low pH balance of 4-5.5), moisturizing, shampoo and conditioner. Don't forget to comb through first.

3. Tie your child's hair each night with a silk scarf, as it keeps the wear and tear from a wild night's sleep from affecting the hair poorly. If you keep finding the scarf on the floor every morning, secure it by putting a stocking cap over it (but never put a stocking cap directly on your child's hair).

4. Never use rubber bands on your child's hair.

5. Never put chemicals on a child's hair under 12 years of age.

6. Use a very minimal amount of gel in the hair as it generally has a high alcohol content (If you must, mix with oil or grease).

If your child is 'tender-headed,' it's important to realize that

NOT combing her/his hair will not be doing her/him a favor, in the long run. Tender-headedness is a result of the scalp not being used to manipulation (which is why, with time and much care, people can become un-tender-headed). Combing regularly is the key to success. When styling your child's hair, **always-always-always** spray it down with the leave-in potion before combing through the hair from ends to roots. *I beg you*- **Please do not get into the habit of styling your child's hair without combing through it** (unless you want locks for your child). Doing this only promotes the forming of mini-locks in the hair, which will be severely traumatic for your little one, should you decide to comb them out.

As for a maintenance schedule, it will vary just a bit. Young hair only needs to be shampooed and conditioned every 2 weeks to 1 month. The only time that you will shampoo on a weekly basis is if your child is swimming (Put <u>grease</u> on the hair when styling, **braid**, and use a plastic cap *under* the swimming cap prior to the session. Shampoo once a week). Make sure to use a clarifying shampoo every 2 weeks to 1 month (2 weeks if swimming 2 or more times a week). Use the same method to shampoo and blow dry that you would use for an adult.

It is really important to remember the 'less is more' rule, when dealing with the kids. Combing and 'fiddling' with your child's hair a lot can lead to mistakes being made. This, of course, can lead to the fall out (the thing that we are *always* trying to avoid). I will go so far as to say that braiding your child's hair and leaving it up for a couple of weeks is the best thing smoking! That way no one is tempted to be touching on, or playing in all of that lovely hair. Just remember not to braid that fragile hair too tightly, because permanent damage can be done by pulling the hair super hard.

Products

- Natural conditioning shampoo and conditioner

- Oil

- Grease

- Leave-in (lotion consistency)

- Leave-in potion (2oz. water, 1oz. cream leave-in, 1oz. oil. Shake well before use)

- Pomade

- Head scarf

- Scrunchies, bows, barrettes, and carefully monitored headbands (watch edges)

Words from the Wise

Celebrity Hairstylist's Chime in on Secrets for Growing Long Hair

I'm so fortunate to have a pool of magical hair masters I can call on to do favors. When I asked a few of my celebrity hairstylist friends and mentors to write down some their best jewels for readers of Long Hair, Do Care, they didn't hesitate. Many thanks to these well respected stylists for giving you the goods they usually reserve for their own clients. I'm sure I can speak for us all, when I say we want to see you with the beautiful head of long, luxurious, hair you desire. My hope is that you will take heed to each valuable tidbit they have offered up. These hair wizard, love bunny, coif slangin', dynamos have affected me in one way or another on my adventures in Hairy Tale Land. Though they are quite busy, they took time out of their schedules to chime in for lil' ole 'us.' This book would have been incomplete without their input. Here's what the pros have to say!

Shonda Dilliehunt, Bay Area Celebrity Stylist - The legendary San Francisco Bay Area hairstylist/sister-friend who gave me my first professional break into celebrity hairstyling and makeup artistry as her assistant on a slew of the Bay's rap icon E-40's music videos. I can never thank Shonda enough for putting me on and showing me the way. She was very instrumental in setting me on my path to success. This book may not have happened, if she had not given me a break. A genuine hair artist, Shonda is a lady who is true through and through.

"When transitioning from relaxed hair to natural, always

deep condition and keep your hair braided, or as straight as possible (with a hot comb) up to the line of demarcation where the textures differ.

To prevent hair from snapping, always-always keep ends clipped. For new hair to grow, DEAD hair must GO!"

Felicia Leatherwood, Celebrity Natural Hairstylist/Creator of The Detangler Brush- My friend and co-worker at Millennium Salon in Los Angeles (an A+ salon with a crew of top notch hairstylists who styles everybody who's anybody with natural hair in Hollywood). First of all, she's just an all-around great person- caring, sweet, talented, and helpful. She's absolutely amazing at styling and caring for natural hair. I've learned volumes from her, in the short year and some change that we worked together. Felicia is always willing to consult with me and give me input (even now), whenever I call her for advice on any big moves that I want to make. Big ups ladybug!

"The best way to grow long healthy hair is to keep a regimen. That way, your hair gets proper treatment on a regular schedule. One of the main reasons why hair is inconsistent is because we are inconsistent. We change routines and products and hairstyles like the wind. We never commit to anything on a consistent basis. So, it's good to have healthy hair and stick to a routine."

Celebrity Hairstylist KaMaura Eley- *KaMaura is a bomb-ass hairstylist! She and I share a common friend (Joe eXclusive, Celebrity Stylist). We would always end up at lunch, a sushi dinner, or some event at the same time. Always so welcoming, funny, and sweet, she ain't never NOT been 'bout it; bout it' in the celebrity, salon, and set-work hair game. Forever working on a show, Forever doing* *it big. I've always admired her drive and super cool personality. It is my plan to make you proud girlie. You answered the call, KaMaura. I know you didn't have to. Keep doing your thing, mama! ***Smooches****

"Want to know my little secret on growing long hair? Well, I believe in the hooded dryer or a steamer with a plastic cap for 15-20 minutes EVERY time you shampoo your hair. The heat from the dryer opens up the hair strands, so the hair can drink however much it needs, leaving the rest in the plastic cap."

Long Hair, Do Care ULTIMATE Cheat Sheet

So, now we've gotten to the good part! **The Cheat Sheet**. I recommend that your first step into the Long Hair Care Schedule start with either a trim or the big chop. This is an optional step. But, I always feel it's best to start on the right foot. In this case, the right foot means having hair that is as free of split and dead ends as possible. I would hate to have you wasting all of this good treatment on hair that is not going to end up the way that you want it to. Always follow the directions that are listed on the products that you choose. Don't forget that your silk scarf is your best friend in the journey to long, healthy hair. Wear it religiously. When your hair starts to feel dry, apply oil to your hair before tying it down at night. It gives you the hot oil treatment effect on a nightly basis. And we know that moisture and TLC are the keys to success. Remember that a trim only has to be 1/4" every two months. AND… No matter what anyone says, I don't recommend shampooing your hair more than once a week (even if you work out). This is a bi-weekly schedule. But if you go weekly, know that the weeks not mentioned are just 'regular' shampoo and style weeks (minus the extras). Let' GO!

Day 1:

Clarifying Shampoo

Protein Conditioner

Hair Masque

Leave-In

Oil

Trim or Big Chop (optional)

Dry

Style

2 Weeks:

Hair Color (If you color, this would be the week)

Moisturizing Shampoo and Conditioner

Leave-In

Oil

Dry

Style

4 Weeks:

Moisturizing Shampoo and Conditioner (This is where you can mix it up with your choice of color treated products or whatever mash up of shampoo and conditioner you like).

Leave-In

Oil

Dry

Style

6 Weeks:

Trim (optional)

Color (optional)

Shampoo and Condition

Leave-In

Oil

Dry

Style

8 Weeks:

Relax (If you're chemically treated)

Treatment Shampoo (Moisture, Protein, Neutralizing or Color) depending on the state of your hair

Treatment Conditioner (Masque, Protein, Hot Oil or Steam) depending on the state of your hair

Leave-In

Dry

Oil (After you dry, to avoid over doing it)

Trim

Dry

Style

10 Weeks:

Color (optional)

Shampoo and Conditioner (Moisturizing or Color Retention)

Leave-In

Oil

Dry

Style

12 Weeks:

Clarifying Shampoo

Moisturizing Shampoo

Protein Conditioner

Deep Conditioner (Moisture Masque)

Leave-In

Oil

Dry

Style

Closing Acknowledgements

I wouldn't dare close this book without taking a little time to shout out a few extraordinary stylists from the Bay Area. When I was just a young pup, these are the people who made me excited about the beauty industry. They mentored me, and gave me the A-1 standard for which to pattern myself. My REAL list is a bit longer than this. But, I narrowed it down to my top four:

1) My Daddy (Mr. John): My Dad taught me many things. But, for this book, I'll keep it short. He taught me that I could make my knack for hair work for me. He taught me to NEVER half-step, to be a go-getter, to be professional, neat, clean, and thorough. He conditioned me to be confident- That I could do IT (whatever that might be) for myself. Most importantly, he taught me that I didn't need permission to live my dreams. Thanks Daddy (Thanks to my Mama too, because she chose well! Muah*!).

2) Mark Robinson (Of Mark's Barber Shop Richmond, CA): When we were both very young, he was already THE barber to go to in Richmond, CA. My best friend (now Reverend), Erika Godfrey, and me would go and sit in the barber shop and watch him cut all the 'boys in the hoods' hair, for like hours. He was super-fast and super-skilled with the clippers. I would soak up everything I could from him, leave the barber shop, and go practice on my grandfather, my brother, cousins, and anybody else who would let me loose on his head. Back then, I was seriously trying to get my skills up, and I was determined to add barbering to my repertoire. He was (and still is) a very

talented and business savvy man that I got my barbering swag from.

3) Betty Ferguson (Betty Ferg): My cosmetology school instructor/mentor. This lady taught me the importance of- 1) a good cut, 2) of being able to do ALL hair types, 3) of being a COMPLETELY skilled stylist, and 4) about how the products that you use on your client's hair will get you to the results that you want. She would always say, "The magic happens at the shampoo bowl!." She ain't never told a lie! What I loved most about her was that mediocrity was nowhere in her repertoire- *AND*, she was sharp as a tack with those clothes... EVERYDAY! (RIP to her sons Skippy and
Dion).

4) Brownie Simms: Last, but not least. When I say she was *PHENOMENAL*, it's an understatement! Not only was she the DOPEST hairstylist that I had seen in my young life, she used to murder the hair extensions
game (*waaaay* before it was a common thing)! What I admired most was that all of her clients had beautiful, shiny, hair. She had that 'however do you want it' flavor. If her clients chose to grow their hair long, she would have them looking like something out of a music video (just hang time flowing all over the place). If they wanted that banging weave, she'd have that thing looking like it grew out of their scalp. I would go to her salon and watch her do hair all day, too. I was in absolute awe of her talent. I used to say, "When I grow up, I want to be like Brownie!" In hair shows, she would always come in first place. NOBODY could see her behind that chair! She inspired me to have that constant hunger for perfection. I don't think she ever knew it, or even if she's still doing hair, but she was definitely

one of my hair idols. Just in case she's unaware, let me repeat- Brownie Simms, you are THE UNDISPUTED TRUTH.

References & Resources

Science In Our World: Certainty and Controversy, "How Does Heat Styling Work and Why Is My Hair The Way It Is?", Natasha Vega, December 6, 2012 article

Livestrong.com: What Vitamins & Minerals Promote Hair Regrowth?, Nadia Haris, December 18, 2013 article

NaturallyCurly.com: "The Cuticle is the First Line of Defense for Our Hair", Tonya McKay, May 8, 2009 article

Viviscal.com: "Best Hair Vitamins for Natural Hair Growth", Viviscal Hair Expert, 2016

TheChalkboardMag.com: "50 Reasons to Drink Wheatgrass Everyday", Suzanne Hall, May 13, 2013 article

PhilipKingsley.com: "The Three Stages of the Hair Growth Cycle", Philip Kingsley, 2016

Loxabeuty.com: "Why Children's Hair is Different from Adults", Megan Gage, January 7, 2013 article

SulfateFreeShampoos.org: "Sulfate Free Shampoo List- Top 45 Best Products", Date unknown, Author unknown

DesignEssentials.com: "Hair Structure", Date unknown, Author unknown, copyright 2013 (pg 9 The facts of hair)

HowToMakeYourHairGrowFasterTips.com: "Hair Cuticle 101- The Most Important Part of Your Hair", Renee Price, Date unknown, copyright 2016 (pg Reconstrutor-Shampoo)

Healthaliciousness.com: "Top 10 Foods Highest in Vitamin E", Date unknown, Author unknown, copyright 2008-2016

www.Healthaliciousness.com: "Top 10 Foods Highest in

Vitamin B1", Date unknown, Author unknown, copyright 2008-2016

www.Healthaliciousness.com: "Top 10 Foods Highest in Vitamin B2", Date unknown, Author unknown, copyright 2008-2016

www.Healthaliciousness.com: "Top 10 Foods Highest in Vitamin B3", Date unknown, Author unknown, copyright 2008-2016

www.Healthaliciousness.com: "Top 10 Foods Highest in Vitamin B5", Date unknown, Author unknown, copyright 2008-2016

www.Healthaliciousness.com: "Top 10 Foods Highest in Vitamin B6", Date unknown, Author unknown, copyright 2008-2016

www.Healthaliciousness.com: "Top 10 Foods Highest in Vitamin B12", Date unknown, Author unknown, copyright 2008-2016

www.newbeauty.com: "11 Collagen-Boosting Foods", Brittany Burhop, October 9, 2013

bembu.com: "20 Foods High in Biotin for Healthy Hair and Nails", Date unknown, Author unknown

Superfoodly.com: Top 10 Lis of Foods High In Alpha Lipoic Acid", May 12, 2016, Superfoodly, copyright 2016

Healthaliciousness.com: "Top 10 Foods Highest in Omega 3s", Date unknown, Author unknown, copyright 2008-2016

Healthaliciousness.com: "Top 10 Foods Highest in Vitamin A", Date unknown, Author unknown, copyright 2008-2016

Healthaliciousness.com: "Top 10 Foods Highest in Vitamin D", Date unknown, Author unknown, copyright 2008-2016

Heathline.com: "Can I Use Vitamins for Hair Growth?",

Zohra Ashpari, August 18, 2014

Milady's Standard Cosmetology, Arlene Alpert, Margrit Altenburg, Diane Bailey, September 1, 2002 (shampoo and conditioner)

Felicia Leatherwood

KaMaura Eley

Shonda Dilliehunt

Erika Godfrey

Meredith Harper-Houston

Myla Beale